THIS BOOK BELONG TO

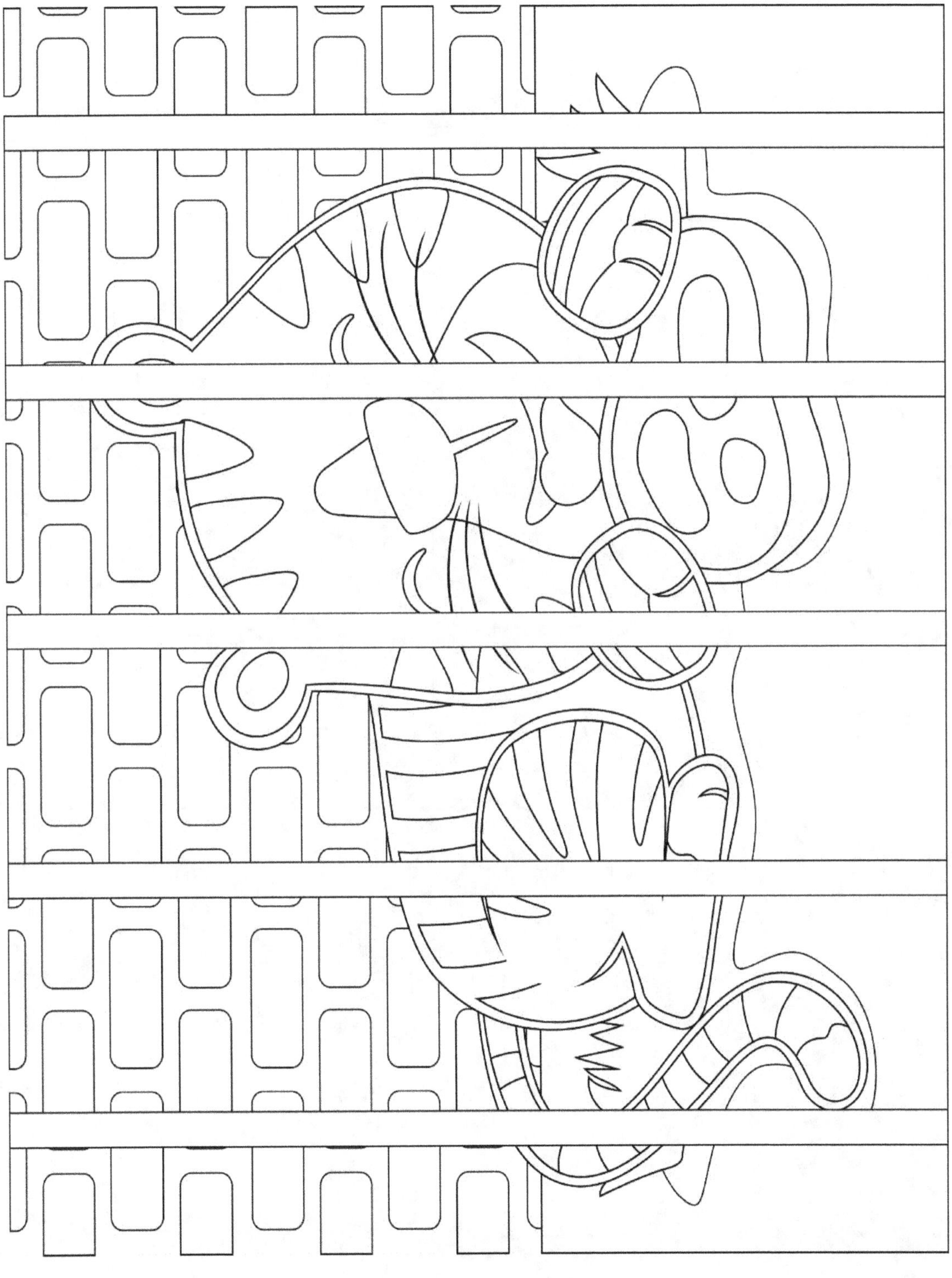

M
RAIL
CROSSING
ROAD
R
R
M
CHOO
CHOO
CHOO..

S

BEACH

Hide & Seek

towel
tooth paste
soap
shampoo

Yummy..

PLAY
GROUND

Travel
choo..
choo..
choo..
M
B

I
banana

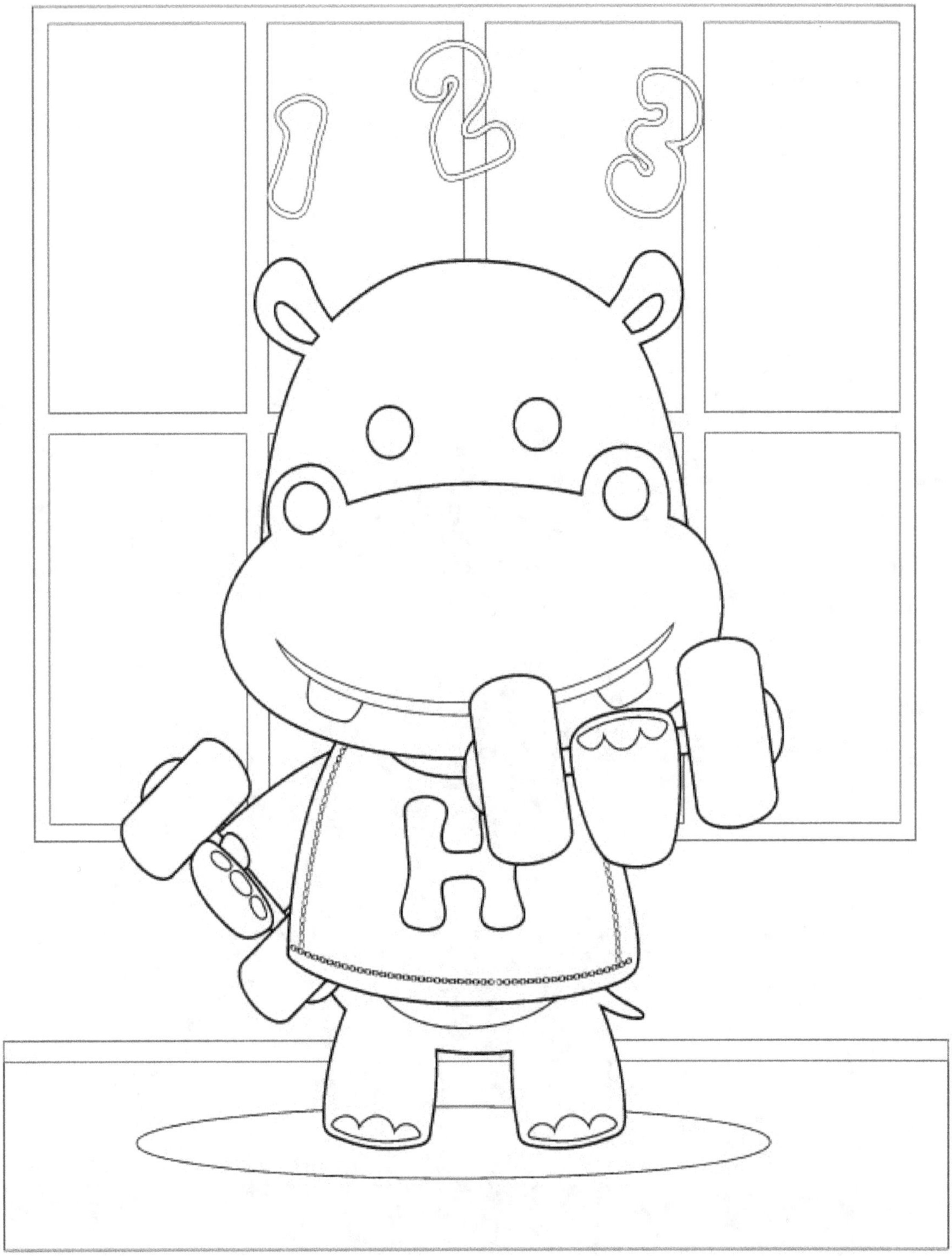
1 2 3
H

G

fishing
time

www.ingramcontent.com/pod-product-compliance
Lightning Source LLC
Chambersburg PA
CBHW080939170526
45158CB00008B/2308
9781080330263